MORRISTOWN CENTENNIAL LIBRARY REGULATIONS

(802) 888-3853

Books and audio cassettes may be kept four weeks unless a shorter time is indicated and may be renewed once for the same period.

A fine of five cents a day every day open will be charged on all overdue library books and audio cassettes. A fine of one dollar a day every day open will be charged for overdue library videos.

No book is to be lent out of the household of the borrower.

All damage to library materials beyond reasonable wear and all losses shall be made good by the borrower.

LIBRARY HOURS

Monday	Closed
Tuesday	10 am-7:30 pm
Wednesday	10 am-7:30 pm
Thursday	10 am-5:30 pm
Friday	10 am-5:30 pm
Saturday	9 am-2 pm
Sunday	Closed

JASON
AND THE
GOLDEN FLEECE

JASON AND THE GOLDEN FLEECE

WRITTEN AND ILLUSTRATED BY

LEONARD EVERETT FISHER

HOLIDAY HOUSE / NEW YORK

The following sources were consulted by the
author in retelling this ancient Greek myth:

Bullfinch, T. *Mythology*. New York: Random
House Inc., Modern Library.
Ceram, C.W. *Gods, Graves, and Scholars*. New
York: Alfred A. Knopf, Inc., 1956.
Graves, R. *The Greek Myths*. volume II, New
York: George Braziller Inc., 1959
Hamilton, E. *Mythology*. Boston: Little, Brown
& Co. Inc., 1940

GREECE

Lemnos

AEGEAN SEA

Iolcos

Corinth

CRETE

Library of Congress Cataloging-in-Publication Data
Fisher, Leonard Everett.
Jason and the golden fleece / written and illustrated by
Leonard Everett Fisher.—1st ed.
p.   cm.
Summary: Jason and his crew of Argonauts set sail on his ship
the Argo in search of the golden fleece.
ISBN 0-8234-0794-2
1. Jason (Greek mythology)—Juvenile literature.   2. Argonauts
(Greek mythology)—Juvenile literature.   [1. Jason (Greek
mythology)   2. Argonauts (Greek mythology)   3. Mythology, Greek.]
I. Title.
BL820.A8F57   1990
398.21—dc20   89-20074   CIP   AC

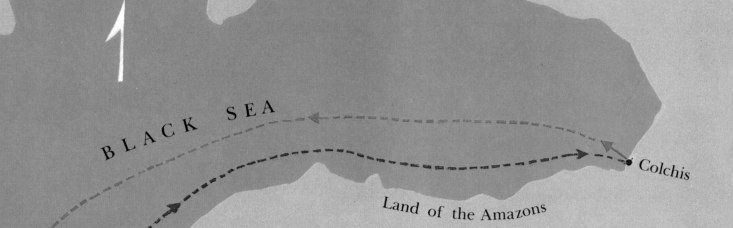

1

BLACK SEA

Colchis

Land of the Amazons

Symplegades

The ancient Greeks believed that gods and goddesses often visited them disguised as humans or animals. Greek stories are filled with adventures of gods and goddesses, monsters and animals, heroes and heroines.

Here is such a tale about a Greek hero, Jason of Iolcos.

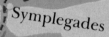

Jason's father, Aeson, should have been King of Iolcos. But the country had fallen into the hands of Jason's evil cousin, Pelias. When Jason grew up he went to the palace. "You have no right to the throne," he said to the king. "It belongs to my father."

King Pelias was sly. He liked being the king. Quickly, he thought of a plan for getting rid of Jason.

"Bring me the golden fleece, and your father shall have his kingdom back," Pelias said. "It is in faraway Colchis. It hangs from a tree in a sacred grove guarded by a sleepless dragon." Turning to his chief adviser, the king whispered, "Jason will never return alive!"

"I shall fetch the golden fleece and lay it at your feet," Jason declared. He was ready for a great adventure.

Jason ordered Argus, the boatbuilder, to construct a sturdy ship, the *Argo*. He then chose fifty of the strongest men of Greece to go with him on the dangerous voyage. They were all sons and grandsons of gods and goddesses. Among them were the twin brothers, Castor and Pollux, who could calm mountainous waves and soothe terrifying winds. He also chose the mighty Heracles, famous throughout Greece for his strength.

With a hot sun above and a flat sea beneath, the Argonauts set sail for Colchis.

Pushed eastward by a stiff breeze and stout oarsmen, the *Argo* sliced through the Aegean Sea. Soon the island of Lemnos rose out of the pink dawn. The Argonauts went ashore for fresh water, food, and rest.

They discovered that there were no men on the island. The women had rebelled and killed all but Thaos, the old king. They had set him adrift in a small boat. Now lonely, the women welcomed the Argonauts and gave them water, food, and fresh clothing.

As the Argonauts left Lemnos, a water nymph flirted with Hylas, Heracles' young servant. When Hylas reached for the lovely nymph she pulled him into the water. Down and down she drew him until they reached the watery deep of her home. Heracles jumped into the sea after his servant.

"Hurry," cried Jason. "We have to leave!"

"Not until I find Hylas!" Heracles yelled.

He refused to quit searching. Jason ordered the *Argo* to sail on, leaving his mighty oarsman stranded in the Aegean Sea.

After several days of hard sailing, the Argonauts landed on another island for a night's rest. There they met Phineus, a starving old man who could predict the future. Once, his predictions had angered Zeus, who did not like anyone to see the future but himself. He punished Phineus by sending nasty, foul-smelling Harpies to eat his meals.

Jason pitied the old man. He ordered two of the Argonauts, sons of the North Wind, to slay the monsters. They stood guard as the shrieking Harpies swooped down to devour Phineus' dinner. But before the brothers could act, the Harpies ate the old man's meal. Carried by their father, the North Wind, the two Argonauts caught the monsters. They were about to kill them when Zeus appeared, saved his "hounds," and ended Phineus' punishment.

Old Phineus then feasted as he had never feasted before. He warned the Argonauts of many dangers ahead like the Symplegades—the crashing rocks guarding the entrance to the Black Sea.

"You will not see them at first," he cautioned. "They are hidden in the mist—two huge rocks ready to roll together and crush your ship between them."

"How shall we sail through them?" Jason asked the old man.

"Send a dove between the rocks," he replied. "If the dove makes it through so will you. But you must be quick. There will be little time."

As the *Argo* and her crew reached the Symplegades, two great rocks loomed out of the mist and closed in on them. Quickly, Jason released a dove. It lost only a few tail feathers as it made it through the rocks safely. The *Argo*'s oarsmen rowed their vessel into the narrow passage. The rocks smashed shut behind them, nipping a few planks from the ship's stern. The slightly damaged ship lurched into the gently rolling Black Sea and continued on her way.

On the other side of the rocks the air was hot and still. The *Argo*'s sail hung limp. Exhausted, the crew slumped over their oars as the ship drifted eastward. Soon they passed the land of the Amazons. Old Phineus had told Jason about this race of warrior goddesses.

"They are daughters of Ares, the God of War," he had warned. "Beware! If you fight them, few of you will survive. Do nothing foolish."

The Argonauts pulled on their oars as the huge sail caught a sharp breeze. The *Argo* quickly slipped past the green hills and sandy beaches as the shouting warrior-women watched them go.

Finally the Argonauts arrived in Colchis, and Jason went to see the king.

"I have come for the golden fleece," he declared.

King Æetes was not about to give up his carefullly guarded treasure. He challenged Jason to complete four impossible tasks. "You shall have your golden fleece only after you yoke two fire-breathing bulls and plow a field. You must sow the furrows with dragon teeth from which will sprout an army that you must defeat—alone"!

Medea, the king's daughter, was a sorceress. As soon as she saw Jason, she fell in love with him and would do anything to help him. "I will give you a magic lotion that will protect you," she told him. "But you must agree to marry me." The lovestruck Jason agreed.

Jason covered himself with Medea's magic lotion and faced the two snorting bulls. Their flaming nostrils heated the air as they trotted around the field, kicking up a thunderous cloud of dust. They wheeled and charged, their flames reaching out and searing his skin. Sidestepping one bull, Jason drove the other to his knees and kept him there. The first bull turned and charged again. Its bronze hooves pounded the hard ground. Jason grabbed him and drove him to his knees, too. With lightning speed he yoked them both.

Next, Jason grooved furrow after furrow, covering the field with straight, shallow trenches. He sowed them with some dragon teeth that Medea had given him. Within minutes hundreds of soldiers rose out of the newly sown field. They headed for Jason!

"Aha!" cried Æetes. "Now he's done for!"

"The stone," Medea said to herself. "Throw the stone!" She had slipped a magic stone to Jason among the dragon teeth. "Toss it in their midst and you will not be harmed," she had whispered to him earlier.

Jason tossed the stone at the oncoming soldiers. They stopped and fought each other until none were left alive. Jason had won. He had proven himself—with the help of Medea's magic.

Medea led Jason to the grove where the dragon guarded the golden fleece. The dragon roared, belching smoke and cinders as they approached. Medea cast a spell over the monster, putting it to sleep. Jason seized the fleece and raced with Medea to the beach where the *Argo* and her crew were waiting. They boarded the ship and set sail for Greece.

King Æetes was enraged. He sent Medea's brother Apsyrtus after the ship. But Apsyrtus and his crew were no match for the *Argo*. They perished at sea.

The *Argo* cut across the Black Sea and again escaped the crashing rocks. Once past Lemnos, she ran into violent storms that drove her south to the coast of Crete. There, as the Argonauts tried to hold the *Argo* steady, a giant made of bronze attacked them.

He hurled huge boulders at the ship. Then he waded into deep water to destroy the *Argo* with his bronze hands. But he sank and drowned.

The danger was over and the *Argo* headed north for home.

Jason returned triumphantly to Iolcos with the golden fleece. He had met King Pelias' challenge. Jason's father, Aeson, could now regain the throne!

But while Jason had been away, King Pelias had made life so unbearable for Aeson that he had killed himself. Jason's mother, Perimede, had died of grief soon after. Torn by sorrow, Jason turned to Medea for help.

"I shall trick Pelias into drinking a magic potion," she promised. "And when he is asleep, I shall persuade his daughters to murder him. I shall tell them that if they kill him, he'll come back to life as a young man."

Medea's plan worked and Pelias was murdered by his daughters. Afterwards, they were furious that they had been tricked. Jason and Medea fled to Corinth, where they married and had two sons.

They were happy for a while. But then Jason fell in love with Glauce, daughter of King Creon of Corinth.

More than anything he wanted to marry her. So he had Medea banished from the city. Jason blamed his change of heart on Aphrodite, Goddess of Love.

"You and Aphrodite used magic to make me fall in love with you," he told Medea, "but now I love Glauce."

"If it were not for my help," protested Medea, "you would not have been able to seize the golden fleece."

Maddened by Jason's betrayal, Medea prepared a dazzling cloak for Jason's bride. When Glauce put it on, her flesh began to burn. She died in agony. Next, Medea murdered her own children, fearing that if they lived, Jason would torment and banish them, too. Jason angrily set out to slay Medea. She escaped in a chariot drawn by winged dragons.

Jason was left with no family or friends. For the rest of his life he wandered all over Greece, alone and homeless.